Wonder CAT

by Irma Singer

illustrated by Elizabeth Wolf

 Harcourt

Orlando   Boston   Dallas   Chicago   San Diego

Y0-DKP-022

2

Kate Cat's cap can go, go, go!
But I am fast. I can save the cap!

I am Wonder Cat. I am brave.
I can save the day.

Ann Ant's hat is on the flag. But I
am brave. I can save the hat.

I am Wonder Cat. I am funny.
I can save the day.

Sam Snake is sad. But I am funny.
I can make Sam Snake glad!

I am Wonder Cat. I am big.
I can save the day.

Dale Duck's cane is stuck. But I am
big. I can save the cane.

I am Wonder Cat. I am never late. I can save the day.

Jack and Jake go down. But I am never late. I can grab Jack and Jake.